# Ginger

## Pupil's Book 4

Early Start Edition – Neubearbeitung
Lehrwerk für Englisch ab Klasse 1

Überarbeitet von
Ulrike Kraaz und Christel Simon

auf der Grundlage der Ausgaben von
Kerstin Caspari-Grote, Ina Grandt,
Birgit Hollbrügge, Ulrike Kraaz,
Claudia Neuber, Christel Simon
und Ines Völtz

Cornelsen

# Contents



**Symbols**

read

listen
CD 1.24

point

talk

act out

## The crew on the ship

**1** Talk about the cabins on the ship.

Abbildungen beschreiben, Wortschatz aus Klasse 3 aktivieren ▸ S. 108

## A postcard from Ginger

**1** Read the postcard. **2** Talk about the pictures.

London

Dear Captain Storm,

I'm in London. It's great.
Please come to London!
Say hello to all the children,
please.

From,
Ginger

To

Captain Storm

Eine Postkarte lesen, über Abbildungen sprechen ▸ S. 113/114

## London sights

CD 1.8 **1** Listen to the CD. **2** Read the text.

**3** Talk about your plans.

This is Big Ben.
It has got a big clock.

This is the London Eye.
You can see London
from the top.

This is Victoria Station.
It's a train station.

This is Tower Bridge.
It's over the River Thames.

This is London Zoo.
There are a lot of animals.

This is Buckingham Palace,
the home of the Royal Family.

## At London Zoo

**1** Talk about the picture.

**2** Read the sentences.

... is climbing / are climbing ...
... is eating / are eating ...
... is drinking / are drinking ...
... is looking at / are looking at ...
... is sleeping / are sleeping ...
... is sitting / are sitting ...

Ein Bild beschreiben, Sätze lesen ▸ S. 125

## Spotlight Landeskunde: A London museum

**1** Read the text.

Madame Tussauds is a museum in London. There are famous people in the museum: pop stars, film stars, sports stars and kings and queens. The people in the museum are made of wax.

**2** Talk.

Emma Watson • Mr Bean • Lady Gaga • Prince William • David Beckham

**3** Make an accordion book of famous people.
*You need: paper, glue, pictures, a round split pin and some string.*

*Fold the paper (like an accordion).*

*Write the name of the book on the cover page and illustrate it. Make a small hole and fix the split pin to the cover page.*

*Glue your pictures into the book.*

*Fix some string around the split pin, so you can close your book.*

## Dick Whittington

**1** Talk about the pictures. **2** Read the story.

Once upon a time there was a boy. His name was Dick Whittington. He was very poor. He lived in a small town.

The next morning Dick was in London.
What a big city! What a big river!
What a lot of big houses! What a lot of big bridges!
But there was no gold on the streets of London.

Bilder beschreiben, eine Geschichte lesen ▸ S. 132

One morning Dick put on his socks. Oh, no! There was a hole in his sock! He put on his shoes. There was a hole in his shoe!

Dick was a good helper in the kitchen.

Now Dick had a penny. He was happy. There was a cat in a shop.

Now Dick had a cat. He was very happy. There was a rat under Dick's bed …

## An invitation from Debbie's brother

**1** Read the text message.

**2** Talk about the pictures.

beach • beach ball • beach towel • bikini • fun park • kite • sea • sunglasses • sun hat • swimming trunks

Eine Textnachricht lesen, Bilder beschreiben ▸ S. 140

## A film crew on the beach

**1** Talk about the picture.

CD 1.23 **2** Listen to the CD. Point.

**3** Read the speech bubbles.

Ein Bild beschreiben, einen Hörtext verstehen und auf die genannten Dinge im Bild zeigen, Sätze lesen ▸ S. 145/146

# Ginger goes to the USA

## On the beach

**1** Talk about the picture.

**2** Read the sentences. Right or wrong?

1. There's a kite in the sea.
2. There's a beach ball on a beach towel.
3. There's a sandcastle under a blue and red kite.
4. There are seashells in the sand.
5. There are two beach balls behind a basket.
6. There's a rucksack in front of Ginger.

**3** Make more sentences.



Ein Bild beschreiben, Aussagen lesen und sie als richtig oder falsch erkennen, eigene Sätze bilden ▸ S. 149

## Sports

**1** Talk about the pictures.

American football • badminton • baseball • basketball • football • table tennis • volleyball

**2** Talk to a partner.

Can you play baseball?

Yes, I can.

No, I can't.

Über die Sportarten auf den Fotos sprechen, sich gegenseitig fragen, ob man eine bestimmte Sportart beherrscht ▸ S. 153/154

## Spotlight Landeskunde: The USA

**1** Read the sentences. Match the pictures.

People from all over the world live in the USA.

People from Ireland:
In March there's a big Irish parade in New York.
Everybody wears green clothes.

People from Germany:
In the picture you can see a German basketball player.

People from China:
This is Chinatown in the USA.

People from Mexico:
You can eat Mexican food everywhere.
Do you like Mexican food?

**2** Make a Mexican wrap.
*You need: a wrap, carrots, cheese, chilli sauce, lettuce, sour cream*

1 Put sour cream and lettuce on your wrap.

2 Put some carrot and cheese on the wrap.

3 Put some chilli sauce on the wrap.

4 Fold your wrap.

Eat your Mexican wrap. Enjoy!



Sich zu den Fotos äußern, Sachtexte lesen und den Fotos zuordnen, ein Rezept lesen und einen Wrap zubereiten ▸ S. 157

## A letter for Captain Storm

**1** Talk about the pictures.

**2** Read the letter.

## At the camping store

**1** Talk about the picture.

CD 1.43 **2** Listen to the CD.

 Über ein Bild sprechen, Preisangaben lesen, einen Hörtext verstehen ▸ S. 165/166

## Spotlight Landeskunde: The Inuit in Canada

**1** Talk about the pictures.

**2** Listen to the CD. Read.

CD 1.49

1

**Nunavut**: Our land
(31 000 people, 85 % Inuit)
**Capital**: Iqaluit

2

Canadian money

3

**The flag of Nunavut**:
North star, Inukshuk,
yellow – soil, white – snow

In Canada, in Nunavut,
The Inuit live there,
The language is Inuktitut,
Nanuq – the polar bear.

4

**Inukshuk**: Man of stone

5

**Animals**: Nanuq – polar bear

**Inuit traditions:**

6

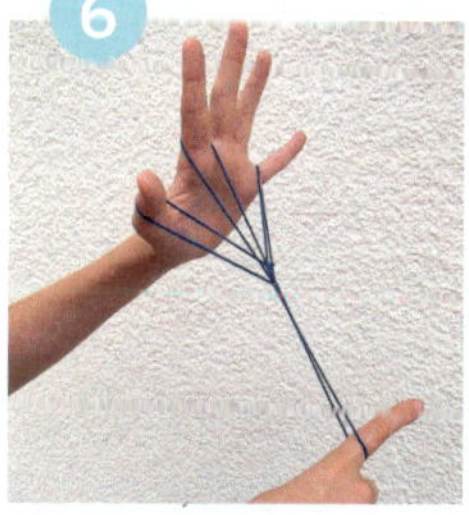

Thread games

7

Throat singing

8

**Transport**: dog sled

**3** Read.

**Languages**: Inuktitut, English
**Transport**: snow mobiles, dog sleds, planes. There are no streets.
**Animals**: polar bear, arctic fox, seal, caribou, whale, walrus
**Inuit traditions**: hunting, fishing, storytelling, throat singing, thread games
**Inuk / Inuit**: man / men
**Asujutilli**: Hello! **Tavvauvutit**: Goodbye.

Über die Abbildungen sprechen, einen Hörtext verstehen,
Informationen über die Kultur der Inuit in Kanada und einen Reim lesen ▸ S. 179/180

## The bear and the beaver

**1** Play the game. Talk to your partner.

Ein Spiel spielen, dabei mit dem Partner sprechen und Sätze lesen ▸ S. 175/176

You need a dice and a counter .

## An e-mail for Colin

**1** Read the e-mail.

**2** Talk about the pictures.

**E-mail**

**RE**: Invitation
**From**: JohnMacDonald@email.com
**To**: ColinBaker@email.com

Dear Colin,
How are you? How's your trip? We're all fine.
My birthday is in three weeks. Please come
to my birthday party. It's at the farm.
All my friends and family will come, too.
Can you all come? Please let me know.

Your friend, John



Eine E-Mail lesen, Bilder beschreiben
▸ S.183/184

## John's birthday

**1** Talk about the picture. Read.

budgie • cat • dog • horse • kangaroo • koala bear

**2** Talk to a partner.

I see something yellow.

Is it the bag?

Yes, it is. / No, it isn't.

**3** Listen to the CD.

CD 2.3

Ein Bild beschreiben und Sätze lesen; Gegenstände nach Beschreibung erraten; einen Hörtext verstehen ▸ S. 185/186

## Tom's daily routine

**1** What time is it?

It's …
… o'clock.
… a quarter past …
… half past …
… a quarter to …

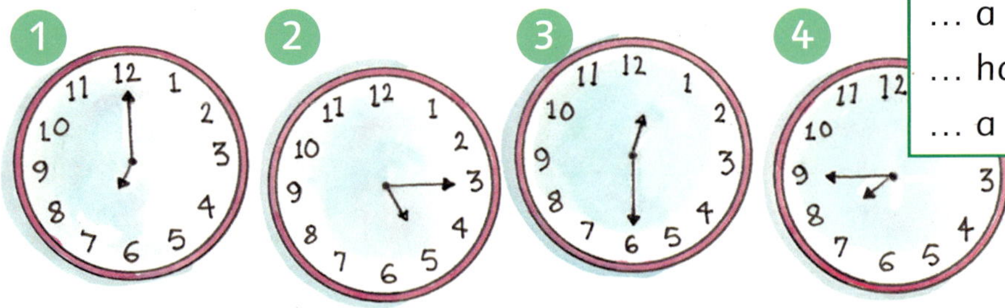

**2** Read about Tom's day.

I get up at 7 o'clock.

I have breakfast at 7.45 a.m.

School lessons start at 9 o'clock.

I have lunch at 12.30 p.m.

I finish school at 3 o'clock.

I help on the farm at 4 o'clock.

I play with my dog at 5.15 p.m.

I have dinner at 6 o'clock.

I go to bed at 8 o'clock.

a.m. → in the morning
p.m. → in the afternoon

**3** Talk about your day.



Über Uhrzeiten und den Tagesablauf sprechen, Sätze lesen und den Abbildungen zuordnen ▸ S. 189/190

## School at home

**1** Talk about the picture. Read Tom's timetable.

| Monday | Tuesday | Wednesday | Thursday | Friday |
|---|---|---|---|---|
| | Reading | Reading | On air private | Reading |
| Maths | Maths On air class | Maths | Maths | |
| Music | | Drama | Science | Music On air class |
| | | **Break** | | |
| English | English | English On air class | | English |
| | | **Lunch** | | |
| Science | Art/Craft | RE | Geography | |
| | | **Break** | | |
| PE | | PE | PE | PE |

**2** Talk to your partner.

Ein Bild beschreiben, einen Stundenplan lesen,
über Schulgegenstände sprechen und jemanden um diese bitten ▸ S. 191/192

## Australian animals

**1** Read about the animals.

This is a wombat.
Wombats are small and strong.
They have small eyes.
Wombats are good swimmers.
They live in holes under the ground.

This is an emu.
Emus are big birds,
but they can't fly.
They have a small head.
Emus have two long legs.
They can run very fast.
Emus live on the ground.

**2** Read and talk about animals.

kangaroo

koala

kookaburra

head
ears
eyes
mouth
nose
legs
feet
toes
tail

| | |
|---|---|
| big | small |
| long | short |

can/can't hop/jump, run, climb, fly

... live on the ground. / under the ground/in holes. / in trees. / in water. / in Australia. / in the mountains. / in caves.



Texte lesen, Tiere und ihre Eigenschaften beschreiben ▸ S. 196

## Spotlight Landeskunde: School of the Air

**1** Talk about the photos. Read.

School of the Air lesson via radio

For School of the Air assemblies pupils give presentations. They sing a song, say a rhyme or read a story.

Pupils on the farm are having a break from the lessons. They are playing outside.

Planes fly to farms in the Outback once a week. The pilot collects and drops off the homework.

**2** Read the timetable. Talk about it.

| | Monday | Tuesday | Wednesday | Thursday | Friday |
|---|---|---|---|---|---|
| 9:00 | Reading<br>On air library | Reading | Reading | Reading | Reading |
| 9:30 | Maths | Maths<br>On air class | Maths | Maths | Maths |
| 10:30 | Music | Art/Craft | Drama | Science | Music<br>On air class |
| 11:00 | | | **Break** | | |
| 11.30 | English | English | English<br>On air class | English | English |
| 12:30 | | | **Lunch** | | |
| 1:30 | Science | Art/Craft | RE | Geography | Drama |
| 2:30 | | | **Break** | | |
| 2:40 | PE | PE | PE | PE | PE |

On air private (30 minutes): Thursday

Informationen über die *School of the Air* im australischen Outback verstehen, über die Fotos sprechen, Texte lesen, den Stundenplan lesen und darüber sprechen ▸ S. 201/202

# Ginger goes to South Africa

## A message for Dr Heal

**1** Talk about the pictures.

CD 2.13 **2** Listen to the CD. Read the message for Dr Heal.

Über Bilder sprechen, eine Nachricht hören, verstehen und lesen ▸ S. 205

## Welcome to Rivertown

CD 2.14

**1** Listen. Where's the clinic, the school and Thabo's house?

Nurse Nombeko

Thabo

Grandma

Dr Heal

## Check-ups in Thabo's school

**1** Read the sentences.

CD 2.15-2.19

**2** Listen to the CD. What's wrong here?

1

2

3

4

5

Abbildungen beschreiben, Sätze lesen, einen Hörtext verstehen, sagen, was auf den Bildern nicht stimmt ▸ S. 212

## At the clinic

**1** Talk about the children. *Elsa has got …*

**2** Read the dialogue. Match the pictures.

Dr Heal: Hello, Thabo.
What's wrong with you?
Thabo: I've got a tummy ache.
Dr Heal: Let me have a look.
Here's some medicine for you.
Thabo: Thank you. Goodbye.
Dr Heal: You're welcome. Goodbye.

1

2

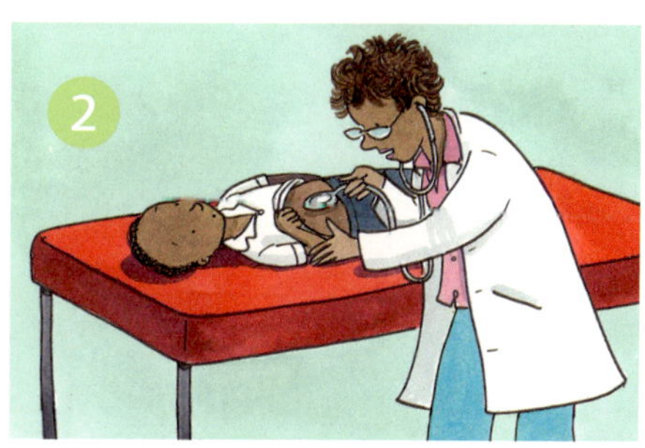

**3** Act out the dialogue with a partner.

Ein Bild beschreiben, einen Dialog lesen,
Sätze Abbildungen zuordnen, eine Szene nachspielen ▸ S. 215/216

## The tortoise had a dream

CD 2.24

**1** Listen to the story. Talk about the pictures.

**2** Read the story.

**3** Act out.

Eine Geschichte hören und verstehen, Bilder beschreiben, die Geschichte lesen und nachspielen ▸ S. 219/220

## Spotlight Landeskunde: Animals in South Africa

**1** Talk about the picture.

CD 2.26

**2** Read the text about the animal. Listen to the CD.

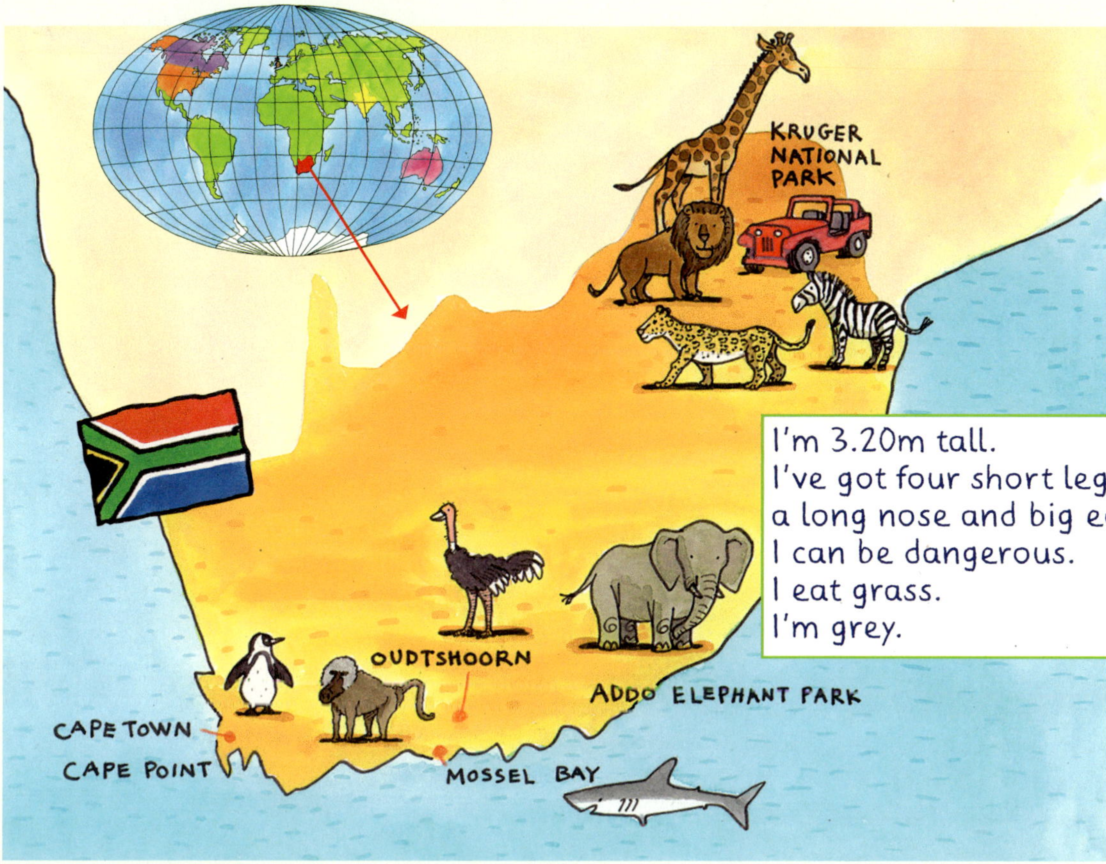


I'm 3.20m tall.
I've got four short legs,
a long nose and big ears.
I can be dangerous.
I eat grass.
I'm grey.

CD 2.25

**3** Listen to the CD. Read the chant.

In Africa, in Africa, there's a lot to see –
Lions, leopards and baboons in a tree.

Elephants, zebras and ostriches, too.
You meet them in nature, not in a zoo.

Penguins, giraffes and sharks in the sea –
Oh, what a wonderful place to be!

Ein Bild beschreiben, einen Text lesen und herausfinden, um welches Tier es sich handelt, Tierbeschreibungen hören und verstehen, einen Chant hören und lesen ▸ S. 223/224

## An e-mail for Ravi

**1** Talk about the pictures.

**2** Read the e-mail.

Über die Abbildungen sprechen, eine E-Mail lesen ▸ S. 227

## Where's Ginger?

1 Talk about the picture. Can you find Ginger?

2 Listen to the CD. 3 Speak the dialogue.

CD 2.30

Ein Bild beschreiben, sagen, wo Ginger sich befindet, einen Hörtext verstehen, einen Dialog sprechen ▸ S. 233/234

## Manu and the snake

**1** Read the story.

**2** Talk. What's missing in the pictures?

**3** Listen to the story.
CD 2.34

1

Manu and his mother were at the market every day. The people and the cows liked Manu's music.

2

3

4

5

Manu put the snake into a basket. Everybody was happy.

6

The snake danced to the music.



Abbildungen beschreiben, eine Geschichte lesen; sagen, was auf den Bildern fehlt, eine Geschichte hören und verstehen ▸ S. 239/240

## At the market

**1** Talk about the pictures. Find 12 differences.

1

2

Bilder beschreiben und zwölf Unterschiede finden ▸ S. 241

## Spotlight Landeskunde: People in India and their jobs

**1** Talk about the pictures.

**2** Listen to the people.

CD 2.35

1 

Ajit

2 

Rajesh

3 

Kiran

4 

Ranga

5 

Sunita

6 

Najuk

**3** Read the speech bubbles.

I'm an elephant trainer but I only work with one elephant. I'm a mahout.

I sing and dance in Bollywood films. They are often about love. I'm an actress.

I'm a taxi driver. But my taxi is not a car. It's a bike! I'm a rickshaw cyclist.

I want to be a cook. And you?

I work with computers. I make new programs and computer games. I'm a computer expert.

I work on a farm. We plant rice. I work 14 hours a day. I'm a paddy farmer.

I work in a clothing factory. I don't go to school. The money is for my family. I'm a factory worker.

Sich zu den Fotos äußern, über Berufe in Indien sprechen, einen Hörtext verstehen, Sätze lesen ▸ S. 243/244

## I hear them

**1** Talk about the pictures.

**2** Sing the song and point to the pictures.

1 

2 

3 clop, clop, clop

4 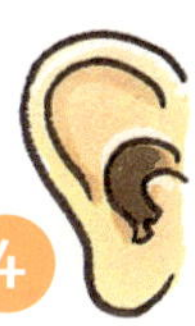

I hear them, I hear them,
I hear them on the roof!
The reindeer are coming.
I hear each prancing hoof.
With a jingle, jingle bell
And a clop, clop, clop.
And a clatter, clatter, clatter
At the chimney top.
I hear them, I hear them,
I hear them on the roof!

5 

6 clatter, clatter, clatter

7 

8 

## An Easter card

**1** Read the sentences. Make your Easter card.

You need: an envelope, a card, scissors, glue, coloured pencils

1



Fold the card.
Open the card.

2

Draw a chicken.

3

Colour the corner red.
Cut off the corner.
It's the beak.

4

Glue the beak on the chicken.
Open the beak.
Fold the card and open it.

5

Draw flowers and grass on your card.

6

Write a message on your card.



Eine Bastelanweisung lesen und verstehen und eine Osterkarte basteln ▸ S. 250

## Remember, remember

**1** Talk about the pictures.

**2** Listen to the rhyme. Read.

CD 2.41

bonfire • fireworks • Guy Fawkes and the three soldiers • Guy Fawkes Night • Houses of Parliament • King James I

### Remember, remember

Remember, remember
the Fifth of November.
Gunpowder, treason and plot.
I see no reason
Why gunpowder treason
Should ever be forgot.

# Goodbye, Ginger!

## Our trip around the world

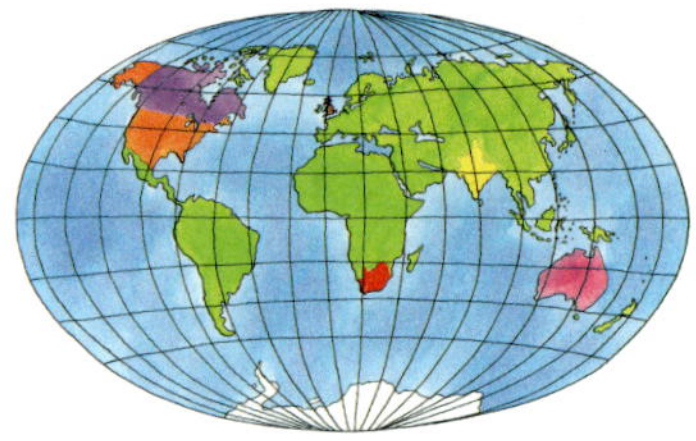

**1** Talk about the pictures.

**2** Read the texts.

*London*

In class 4 we went to London.
Buckingham Palace is the home of the Royal Family.
There are big red buses in the streets.
Ginger is from London. He is our friend.

We went to the USA.
New York is a very big city in the USA.
There were pirates on the beach in Los Angeles.
Debbie Jones is from the USA.
She is the radio operator on our ship.

*The USA*

*Canada*

We went to Canada.
There are a lot of mountains, rivers and lakes there.
There was a fish on Captain Storm's teepee.
Captain Storm is from Canada.
He is the captain on our ship.

We went to South Africa.
There were bikes, chairs and tables on top of the buses.
Thabo had a tummy ache.
Dr Heal is from South Africa.
She is the doctor on our ship.

*South Africa*

*Australia*

We went to Australia.
Australia is very big.
There are kangaroos hopping around.
Colin Baker is from Australia.
He is the cook on our ship.

We went to India.
There are a lot of people and big markets there.
You can see cows in the street.
Ravi Mehta is from India.
He is the mechanic on our ship.

*India*



Bilder beschreiben und Texte lesen ▸ S. 255/256

## A
**a** ein, eine
**a lot of** viel/e
**about** über
**act** Akt, Aufführung
**action** Action, Handlung
**activity** Aktivität
**adjective** Adjektiv
**afternoon** Nachmittag
**again** wieder, noch einmal
**agree** sich einig sein, zustimmen
**all** alle
**all right** in Ordnung
**already** schon
**American football** American Football
**angry** wütend
**animal** Tier
**animal programme** Tiersendung
**anything** etwas
**April** April
**are** sind
**arm** Arm
**at** bei, im, um
**August** August
**aunt** Tante
**Australia** Australien

## B
**back** zurück
**badminton** Federball/ Badminton (Spiel)
**badminton birdie** der Federball
**bag** Tasche
**banana** Banane
**baseball** Baseball
**basket** Korb
**basketball** Basketball
**bathroom** Badezimmer
**be** sein
**beach** Strand
**beach ball** Wasserball
**beach towel** Strandtuch
**beak** Schnabel
**bear** Bär
**beaver** Biber
**because** weil
**bed** Bett
**bedroom** Schlafzimmer
**behind** hinter
**bell** Glocke
**best boy** Assistent (Beleuchtung)
**between** zwischen
**big** groß
**bike** Fahrrad
**bikini** Bikini
**bird** Vogel
**birdie** Federball
**birdcage** Vogelkäfig
**birthday** Geburtstag
**black** schwarz
**blond** blond
**blow up** sprengen, explodieren
**blue** blau
**body** Körper
**book** Buch
**bonfire** Lagerfeuer
**boomerang** Bumerang
**boring** langweilig
**bottle** Flasche
**bowl** Schale
**box** Kasten
**boy** Junge
**break** Pause
**breakfast** Frühstück
**bridge** Brücke
**British** britisch
**brown** braun
**budgie** Wellensittich
**buffalo** Büffel
**bus** Bus
**bus stop** Bushaltestelle
**bush** Strauch, Busch
**busy** beschäftigt
**but** aber
**buy** kaufen
**by (go by bus)** mit (mit dem Bus fahren)

## C
**camera** Kamera, Fotoapparat
**camera man** Kameramann
**camp** Lager, Camp
**camping** Zelten
**camping store** Campinggeschäft
**can** können
**Canada** Kanada
**car** Auto
**card** Karte
**careful** vorsichtig
**carpet** Teppich
**carrot** Mohrrübe
**cartoon** Zeichentrickfilm
**cat** Katze
**cave** Höhle
**CD player** CD-Spieler
**centimetre** Zentimeter
**chair** Stuhl
**cheese** Käse
**chicken** Huhn
**child** Kind
**children** Kinder
**chimney** Kamin, Schornstein
**Christmas** Weihnachten
**city** Stadt
**clapper** Materialassistent (Kamera)
**class** Klasse
**clean** saubermachen
**clear** klar, deutlich
**climb** klettern
**clinic** Klinik
**clock** Uhr
**clothes** Kleidung
**coconut** Kokosnuss
**coin** Münze
**cold** 1. kalt 2. Erkältung
**collect** sammeln
**colour** 1. Farbe 2. (aus)malen
**colour in** ausmalen
**coloured pencil** Buntstift
**come** kommen
**come up** aufgehen (Sonne)
**comic** Comic(heft)
**computer** Computer
**computer game** Computerspiel
**cookie** Keks
**corner** Ecke
**correct** richtig
**cough** Husten
**count** zählen
**counter** Spielstein
**country** Land
**cow** Kuh
**crayon** Stift
**crocodile** Krokodil
**crocus** Krokus
**cross** überqueren
**cut off** abschneiden

## D
**dad** Papa
**daffodil** Narzisse
**dangerous** gefährlich
**day** Tag

# Word list

**December** Dezember
**dice** Würfel
**dingo** Dingo
**dinner** Abendessen
**director** Regisseur, Chef
**do** machen
**doctor** Arzt/Ärztin
**dog** Hund
**dollar** Dollar
**down** herunter, unten
**downstairs** unten
**draw** zeichnen
**dream** Traum
**drink** trinken
**duck** Ente

## E

**eagle** Adler
**earache** Ohrenschmerzen
**Easter** Ostern
**Easter egg** Osterei
**eat** essen
**egg** Ei
**eighty** achtzig
**elephant** Elefant
**else** sonst, sonst noch
**emu** Emu
**enjoy** genießen
**envelope** Briefumschlag
**every** jede/r/s
**everybody** alle
**excuse** entschuldigen
**eye** Auge

## F

**family** Familie
**famous** berühmt
**farm** Bauernhof, Farm
**fast** schnell
**father** Vater
**Father Christmas** Weihnachtsmann
**February** Februar
**feed** füttern
**feet** Füße
**fifty** fünfzig
**film** Film
**film crew** Filmteam
**find** finden
**find out** herausfinden
**finish** 1. Schluss 2. aufhören, beenden
**fireworks** Feuerwerk
**fish** Fisch
**fitness** Fitness
**flag** Flagge
**flower** Blume
**flute** Flöte
**fly** fliegen
**fold** falten
**food** Essen
**foot** Fuß
**football** Fußball
**for** für
**forget** vergessen
**forty** vierzig
**freckle** Sommersprosse
**free** frei, kostenlos
**friend** Freund/in
**from** von
**fruit** Obst
**full** voll
**full of** voller
**fun** Spaß
**funny** lustig

## G

**Germany** Deutschland
**get** werden, bekommen
**get up** aufstehen
**giraffe** Giraffe
**girl** Mädchen
**give** geben
**glass** Glas
**glasses** Brille
**glue** 1. Kleber 2. kleben
**go** gehen
**go camping** zelten gehen
**go down** untergehen
**gold** Gold
**good** gut
**goose** Gans
**grandpa** Opa
**grass** Gras
**Great Britain** Großbritannien
**green** grün
**greeting** Gruß
**ground** Boden
**guinea pig** Meerschweinchen
**gunpowder** Schießpulver
**guy** Kerl

## H

**hair** Haar
**half** halb
**half past** eine halbe Stunde nach
**hamburger** Hamburger
**hamster** Hamster
**happy** glücklich
**have got** haben
**has got** hat
**have** haben
**have a picnic** picknicken
**have lunch** zu Mittag essen
**head** Kopf
**headache** Kopfschmerzen
**height** Höhe, Größe
**help** helfen
**helper** Helfer
**her** ihr/e
**here** hier
**his** sein/e
**hole** Loch
**holidays** Ferien
**home** Haus, Zuhause
**homework** Hausaufgaben
**honey** Honig
**hoof** Huf
**hop** hüpfen
**hope** hoffen
**hot** heiß
**house** Haus
**how** wie
**hundred** hundert
**hungry** hungrig

## I

**I** ich
**idea** Idee
**illness** Krankheit
**in** in
**in front of** vor
**India** Indien
**information** Information
**instruction** Anweisung
**interesting** interessant
**into** in (... hinein)
**is** ist
**it** es

## J

**January** Januar
**job** Arbeit
**July** Juli
**jump** hüpfen
**June** Juni
**just** nur

## K

**kangaroo** Känguru
**kill** töten
**kitchen** Küche
**kite** Drachen

**knee** Knie
**know** wissen, kennen
**koala** Koala
**kookaburra** Kookaburra

## L

**lake** See
**left** links
**leg** Bein
**lesson** Schulstunde, Lektion
**let** lassen
**letter** Brief, Buchstabe
**light** Licht
**like** mögen
**line** 1. Reihe, Zeile 2. Linie
**listen (to)** zuhören
**live** leben
**living room** Wohnzimmer
**long** lang
**look** schauen, sehen
**look at something** sich etwas ansehen
**loud** laut
**luck** Glück
**lunch** Mittagessen

## M

**magazine** Zeitschrift
**maize** Mais
**make** machen
**man** Mann
**map** Landkarte
**March** März
**market** Markt
**market stand** Marktstand
**May** Mai
**me** mich, mir
**meet** treffen
**medicine** Medizin
**melon** Melone
**message** Nachricht
**metre** Meter
**microphone** Mikrofon
**mine** mein, meiner, meines
**minute** Minute
**mobile phone** Handy
**money** Geld
**monkey** Affe
**month** Monat
**moose** Elch
**morning** Morgen
**mother** Mutter
**mountain** Berg
**mouse** 1. Maus 2. Computermaus
**mouth** Mund
**move** bewegen
**much** viel
**mud** Schlamm
**mum** Mama
**music** Musik
**music show** Musiksendung

## N

**name** Name
**narrator** Erzähler
**never** nie
**new** neu
**next** nächster, nächste
**next to** bei, neben
**nice** schön, nett
**night** Nacht
**ninety** neunzig
**nose** Nase
**not** nicht
**November** November
**now** jetzt
**number** 1. Nummer 2. nummerieren
**nurse** Krankenschwester

## O

**o'clock** Uhr
**October** Oktober
**old** alt
**on** an, auf
**onion** Zwiebel
**only** nur
**on top** oben, auf
**open** 1. öffnen, 2. offen
**ostrich** Vogel Strauß
**our** unser, unsere
**out of** aus, von
**over** über

## P

**page** Seite
**palace** Palast
**paper** Papier
**paper cup** Pappbecher
**paper towel** Papierhandtuch
**past** nach
**peanut** Erdnuss
**peanut butter** Erdnussbutter
**pen** Füller
**pencil** Bleistift
**pencil case** Federmappe
**pencil sharpener** Bleistiftspitzer
**people** Menschen, Leute
**pet** Haustier
**picnic** Picknick
**picture** Bild
**pineapple** Ananas
**pirate** Pirat
**play** spielen
**player** Spieler
**please** bitte
**plot** Verschwörung
**pocketbook** Taschenbuch
**pocket knife** Taschenmesser
**police officer** Polizist
**poor** arm
**postcard** Postkarte
**pot** Kanne, Topf
**potato** Kartoffel
**pound** Pfund
**presentation** Präsentation
**press-up** Liegestütz
**programme** Programm
**puddle** Pfütze
**put** setzen, stellen, legen

## Q

**quarter** viertel
**queen** Königin
**quiz show** Ratesendung

## R

**rabbit** Kaninchen
**rat** Ratte
**read** lesen
**ready** fertig
**red** rot
**reindeer** Rentier
**remember** erinnern
**repeat** wiederholen
**rhyme** Reim
**rice** Reis
**rich** reich
**right** rechts
**river** Fluss
**rock** Stein
**role-play** Rollenspiel
**roll** rollen
**roof** Dach
**room** Zimmer
**royal** königlich
**rubber** Radiergummi
**rubbish** Abfall
**rucksack** Rucksack
**ruler** Lineal
**run** rennen

## S

**sad** traurig
**sand** Sand
**sandal** Sandale

# Word list

**sandcastle** Sandburg
**say** sagen
**school** Schule
**scissors** Schere
**sea** Meer
**seashell** Muschel
**seat** Sitz, Platz
**see** sehen
**sentence** Satz
**September** September
**seventy** siebzig
**shark** Hai
**sheep** Schaf/e
**shirt** Hemd
**shoe** Schuh
**shop** Geschäft, Laden
**shop assistant** Verkäufer/-in
**short** 1. kurz 2. klein
**shoulder** Schulter
**show** Aufführung
**sight** Sehenswürdidkeit
**sister** Schwester
**sixty** sechzig
**skirt** Rock
**sleep** schlafen
**sleeping bag** Schlafsack
**sleepy** schläfrig
**sleigh** Schlitten
**small** klein
**snow** Schnee
**sock** Socke
**sofa** Sofa
**soldier** Soldat
**some** etwas
**something** etwas
**sometimes** manchmal
**song** Lied
**soon** bald
**sore throat** Halsschmerzen
**sound operator** Toningenieur
**sour cream** Sauerrahm
**South Africa** Südafrika
**speak** sprechen
**sports** Sport
**sports programme** Sport-sendung
**stamp** Briefmarke
**stand** stehen
**start** 1. Beginn, Anfang 2. beginnen, anfangen
**station** Bahnhof
**stone** Stein
**stop** 1. stoppen, aufhören, 2. Haltestelle
**storeroom** Vorratskammer
**straight** gerade
**straight on** geradeaus
**street** Straße
**strong** stark
**sun** Sonne
**sunglasses** Sonnenbrille
**sun hat** Sonnenhut
**sweet potato** Süßkartoffel
**swim** schwimmen
**swimmer** Schwimmer
**swimming trunks** Badehose

## T

**table tennis** Tischtennis
**tail** Schwanz
**take** nehmen
**take off** ausziehen
**tall** groß
**tea** Tee
**teepee** Tipi
**tent** Zelt
**text** Text
**text message** SMS
**that** der, die, das
**the** der, die, das
**there** dort
**they** sie (Mehrzahl)
**thirty** dreißig
**think** denken
**throw** werfen
**tick** abhaken
**ticket** Fahrschein
**ticket machine** Fahrkarten-automat
**time** Zeit
**timetable** Stundenplan
**tired** müde
**to** nach, zu
**toe** Zeh
**toilet** Toilette
**top** oben
**torch** Taschenlampe
**tortoise** Schildkröte
**touch** berühren
**town** Stadt
**track** Spur
**train** Zug
**travel** reisen
**treasure chest** Schatzkiste
**tree** Baum
**trousers** Hose
**tulip** Tulpe
**tummy** Bauch
**tummy ache** Bauchweh
**turn** abbiegen, umdrehen
**turn around** umdrehen, wenden
**TV** Fernseher
**twenty-one** einundzwanzig
**twin** Zwilling

## U

**uncle** Onkel
**under** unter
**underground** 1. unter der Erde, 2. U-Bahn
**underline** unterstreichen
**up** oben, auf, herauf
**upstairs** oben
**USA** Vereinigte Staaten von Amerika

## V

**vegetable** Gemüse
**very** sehr
**visit** 1. Besuch, 2. besuchen
**volleyball** Volleyball

## W

**walk** gehen
**want** wollen, möchten
**watch** 1. Armbanduhr 2. zusehen, zuschauen
**water** Wasser
**water bottle** Wasserflasche
**watermelon** Wassermelone
**we** wir
**wear** anhaben, tragen
**week** Woche
**welcome** 1. Willkommen, 2. begrüßen
**well** gesund, gut
**what** was
**where** wo, wohin
**white** weiß
**who** wer
**why** warum
**with** mit
**wolf** Wolf
**wombat** Wombat
**word** Wort
**world** Welt
**world map** Weltkarte
**write** schreiben
**wrong** falsch

## Y

**year** Jahr
**yellow** gelb
**your** dein
**Yuck!** Igitt!